D1613833

The Proust Questionnaire

Thanks to the House of Gérard Darel,
owner of the original edition of the Proust Questionnaire.

Foreword by William C . Carter • Introduction by Henry-Jean Servat

The Proust
Questionnaire

ASSOULINE

Foreword

In writing the recent biography *Marcel Proust: A Life,* I attempted to show how Proust, generally considered by his peers a talented but frivolous dilettante, came to produce what is arguably the most brilliant sustained prose narrative in the history of literature. Books about Proust and his work, as well as adaptations of *In Search of Lost Time* for the stage and screen, continue to proliferate. Why does Proust remain such a presence among us? Why is he still very much our contemporary? Perhaps more than any other writer of fiction, Proust explores, probes, and analyzes the human psyche in its conscious and unconscious manifestations. His novel, like the psychological and scientific contributions of his distinguished contemporaries Sigmund Freud and Albert Einstein, is innovative and bold, showing us aspects of the human personality that had never been so closely examined and rendered in such rich and fascinating detail. Joseph Conrad saw Proust's insatiable curiosity, his endless investigations of what it is to be human as the key to his genius: Proust's work is "great art based on analysis." Conrad remarked, "I don't think there is in all creative literature an example of the power of analysis such as this."

Like Einstein, Proust provided a new vision of the universe in which relativity and multiple perspectives were distinctive features. Edmund Wilson went so

Portrait of Marcel Proust as a young teenager, by Horst Janssen.

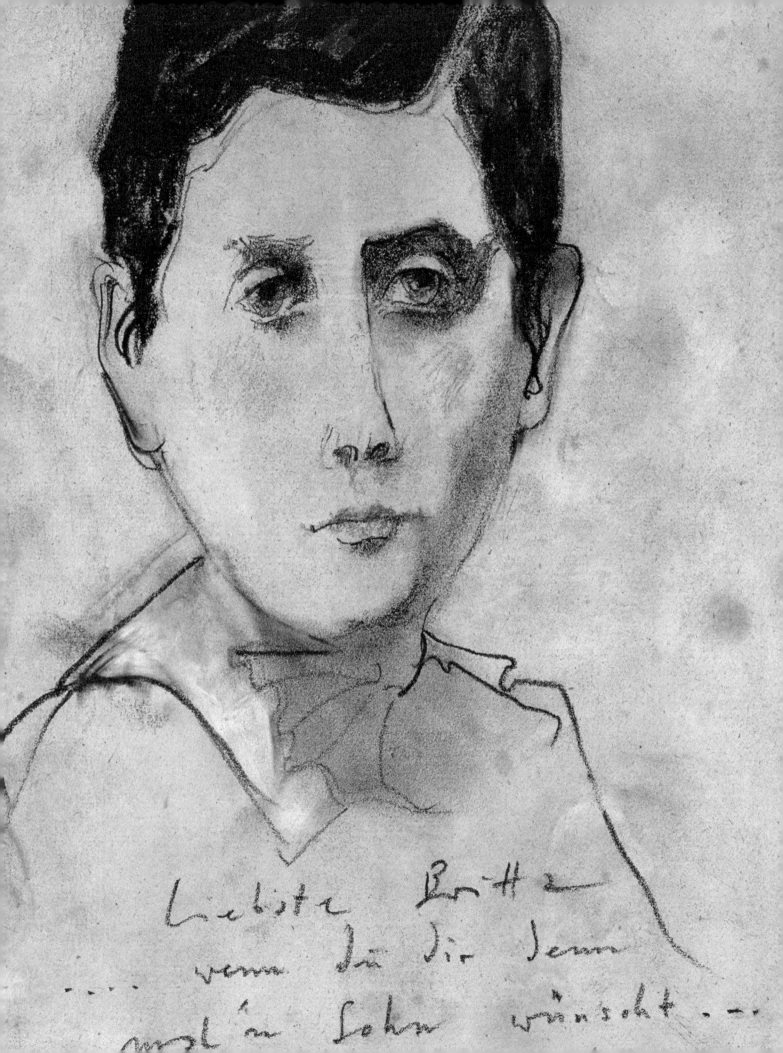

Liebste Britta
..... wenn du dir denn
mal 'n Sohn wünscht ...

far as to declare *In Search of Lost Time* the literary equivalent of Einstein's theory: "Proust has re-created the world of the novel from the point of view of relativity: he has supplied for the first time in literature an equivalent on the full scale for the new theory of physics." *In Search of Lost Time* continues to speak to generation after generation in a voice that remains fresh and vigorous. Far from being the culminating opus of decadent literature, as some early critics believed, this novel constitutes one of the most dynamic texts ever written, whose tremendous energy acts as a rejuvenating force. All its narrative elements—plot, characters, style, and so forth—create, as Iris Murdoch said of its effect, "the most intense pleasure one does find in great art." We call this pleasure "aesthetic," whose root meaning is to feel, to be alive. Virginia Woolf, the legendary writer, identified the highly sensual nature of Proust's prose and what one might call the "Proustian effect," which explains the appeal of his novel to the many readers who become hooked on it. "Proust so titillates my own desire for expression that I can hardly set out the sentence. Oh if I could write like that! I cry. And at the moment such is the astonishing vibration and saturation and intensification that he procures —there's something sexual in it—that I feel I *can* write like that, and seize my pen and then I *can't* write like that. Scarcely anyone so stimulates the nerves of language in me: it becomes an obsession."

Woolf's reaction to *Swann's Way* anticipated what Proust describes in *Time Regained* as the artist's goal—and what our own pursuit should be: to live in such heightened awareness by leading "the true life," by marshaling, invigorating, and deploying our own remarkable talents. *In Search of Lost Time* is also one of the great comic works in literature—comedy of the highest order that amuses, delights, and frequently dazzles as it instructs. Not only do great works contain tremendous rejuvenating energy, their effect is even consoling. The ultimate product of *In Search of Lost Time* is joy. Proust's novel, in spite of its innovative nature and unprecedented scale, quickly found its public. Now, nearly a century later, its popularity endures and expands. It has been never been out of print and exists in approximately forty translations. This book has created, as Proust noted that all works of genius ultimately do, its own posterity. What he admiringly wrote about Beethoven's late quartets applies just as well to *In Search of Lost Time*: "The reason why a work of genius is not easily admired from the first is that the man who has created it is extraordinary, that few other men resemble him. It is his work itself that, by fertilising the rare minds capable of understanding it, will make them increase and multiply." Like Beethoven, and like Virginia Woolf, Proust remains a vital and nourishing presence among us.

William C. Carter
*University of
Alabama at Birmingham*

A Question of Marcel Proust

Lowering his small head, he picked up a black ink pen and began to write. Marcel, the eldest son of Doctor Adrien Proust, was 15. He attended the Lycée Condorcet in Paris, where, with just the right amount of enthusiasm not to be labeled a bad pupil, he embarked on his studies in Latin, Greek, and Biology. During classes, he would pass elaborately worded love notes to his friends, usually to boys. With his pale complexion, dark gaze, and spirited manner, he was attracted only to those of similar appearance. Imbued with a great ideal of happiness, he would spend his time dreaming. Although he usually went to bed late, he still could not fall asleep without a kiss from his mum. It was 1886, and Baron Haussmann had just inaugurated his splendid boulevards starting from the Arc de Triomphe, renovating the city of Paris. The bourgeois buildings now flanking these boulevards housed huge apartments with parquet floors and stucco ceilings, water taps, gas lighting, central heating, and modern lifts.

The Proust family—the doctor, his wife, Jeanne, Marcel, and the youngest Robert, plus a few servants—lived at number 9, boulevard Malesherbes. Due to the inhalations Marcel required for his asthma, the smell of eucalyptus not only pervaded his bedroom but spread to the adjoining rooms. The young boy, overprotected by those around him, had become accustomed to this secure and pampered world. Outside, in the magnificent quartiers, it was a Paris of horse-drawn buses, elegant carriages, balls held at the Opéra, creatures adorned with ostrich feathers and diamond sprays, and gentlemen in tailcoats. The Eiffel Tower, then under construction, served as a backdrop for nannies and children playing on the pristine avenues off the Bois de Boulogne or on the carefully manicured lawns along the Champs-Elysées. And in this setting of dandies prancing around under the gaze of pretty women and hackneys trotting up and down, the young Marcel began to form amorous friendships. It was the summer of 1886, when he turned 15, that marked his journey into adolescence. The transformation was over in no time at all, as it was with most of his friends at the time. Among Proust's favorite playtime companions were Marie and Nelly de Benardaky, whose father had been the master of ceremonies at the Imperial Court of the czar. Marcel's affection for Marie (who would later marry Prince Michel Radziwill) probably served as a model for the feelings that the narrator of *In Search of Lost Time* would later show toward his heroine Gilberte. At this time, Marcel also struck up a friendship with a girl called Antoinette, the daughter of Félix Faure, then deputy, and eventually president of the Republic. The young gray-eyed girl wore a feathered hat, carried a sunshade, and kept with the fashion of the day, by having a sort of personal diary. The book took the form of a small, flat, arabesque-studded red leather album that her governess bought in the Galignani bookshop, which specialized in the sale of American and English works and is located in the rue de Rivoli arcade. This kind of album from Victorian England was highly valued at the time by a bourgeois society in favor of an anglophile France.

Entitled *Confessions. An Album to Record Thoughts, Feelings, etc.,* the book was an account of the dreams and hopes of rich turn-of-the-century grandchildren. Each page contained the same questionnaire, which consisted of twenty-four questions. The answers they elicited were supposed to provide insight into the inner soul of the participant by revealing his or her hidden feelings. Little Antoinette used to lend her album, printed in the language of Shakespeare, to her friends, whom she and her sister, Lucie, would receive for afternoon tea, then a fashionable society custom. The friends would join in the game, all the rage in 1886, answering each personal question from the given list in French between mouthfuls of madeleine and gulps of tea. Eventually, it came to the turn of the young Marcel Proust, who approached the task with great care. He was one of the last to undergo this familiar test, but also one of the few not to sign his name. Out of the twenty-four questions, he replied to only twenty. The young Marcel chose not to disclose his "main attribute," "favorite names," the "historical characters [he despised] the most," nor his "current state of mind."

The most surprising thing about this tale, and the most important, as it sheds light on the personality of one of the greatest writers of his century, is that this questionnaire album has remained intact despite the upheaval and turmoil of subsequent decades. Carefully filed away by its owner, it was preserved from the ravages of time. At the Marcel Proust exhibition in 1965 at the Bibliothèque Nationale in Paris, the journal was item number 59, entitled "Antoinette Faure's album" and exhibited as a belonging of Doctor André Berge, Antoinette's husband. In fact, in 1924 one of his descendants discovered the red notebook in a dusty trunk in his attic, in the middle of what the latter described as "the heap of volumes transformed by humidity into a kind of sticky paste that formed a bond between the few pitiful survivors." The cover was dated 1884, and other dates are mentioned at various stages throughout the book, which ends in 1887. In the "Cahier du mois no. 7," written on December 1, 1924, two years after Proust's death, André Berge related his discovery under the title "About a Lucky Find." After visiting the writer's younger brother, Doctor Robert Proust, he wrote: "The confession I have in my possession was written by Marcel Proust at the age of 13 or 14. Monsieur Robert Proust was unable to show me any specimen of his brother's handwriting at this age, but together we analyzed several pages of more recent writing, where we found a large number of handwritten characters that were already clearly illustrated in the red book. And in any case, anyone who knew Marcel Proust as a child could not fail to recognize him by his reply to the question "What, for you, is the depth of misery?" Proust wrote, "Being separated from Mum!" At first he had written "being away from Mother!" but what is really so bad about being away?

It is an acquired idea and one that is only painful on reflection. No, the depth of misery for this young passionate boy was separation, that harsh reality we experience directly, intensely, almost physically. And with this cross-out, and substitution of the words "away from" with the word "separated," we can surely recognize the everlasting unease of this great psychologist who, with his subtle turns of phrase, strived to reflect the most elusive nuances of thought no matter what. I found evidence of this uneasiness in almost every line. For example: to the question "Where would you like to live?" Proust replied, "In an ideal, or rather my ideal country." The stupid questions in the album would have required conclusive answers, too uncouth to be exact. But a master with words like Proust knew how to get out of a trap like this. And he escapes either by remaining silent and not answering, or by doing the opposite and producing long lists or general ideas. On several occasions in this confession, he mentions Augustin Thierry, one of the great French masters of romantic historiography. That worried me, although for Robert Proust it was just one more piece of evidence. "Our grandmother was completely taken with Augustin Thierry and spoke about him nonstop," he told me. "She had communicated this devotion to Marcel, and I really do not believe there are many other children of 13 or 14 who would choose Augustin Thierry as their favorite prose writer."

André Berge's story was followed by the young Marcel's replies to the questionnaire in the album. These replies compose the first of Proust's "confessions," published in full, without alteration or omission. It was accompanied by a reproduction of the cover and the facsimile of a page from the album. Put up for auction at Drouot in Paris in 2003, it was purchased by Gérard Darel, owner of the eponymous ready-to-wear house and a great admirer of Marcel Proust.

As an adult, the young Marcel would never tire of dipping his pen in inkwells or filling pages with his writing. At age 20, having completed his military service, he took to this game once more and replied a second and last time to what would become known as "Proust's Questionnaire."

The collection of handwritten replies to the later questionnaire comprises the second of Proust's "confessions," published in *La Revue illustree XV* in 1892, in the piece entitled "Salon Confidences written by Marcel." Also christened, if not engraved, with the title "Proust's Questionnaire," it is often confused with the first version. However, seven additional questions distinguish the latter from the former. And the difference between Marcel's replies in the two questionnaires bear witness to the blossoming development and confirmation of his tastes, particularly aesthetic and sexual.

However they may vary in form, undergo cuts, and give rise to digressions, "Proust's Questionnaire" remains one of the most popular methods of interview used by media throughout the world, enjoying exceptional and indisputable renown.

Henry-Jean Servat

Cover of the original *Confessions. An Album to Record Thoughts, Feelings…* (lifesize).

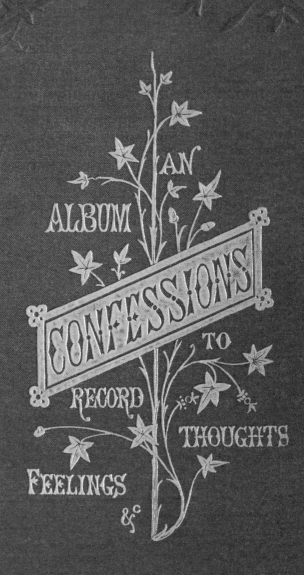

AN
ALBUM
CONFESSIONS
TO
RECORD
THOUGHTS
FEELINGS
&c

Your favourite virtue. All virtues that are not limited to a sect: the universal virtues.

Your favourite qualities in man. Intelligence, moral sense.

Your favourite qualities in woman. Gentleness, naturalness, intelligence.

Your favourite occupation. Reading, dressing, writing verse, history, theater.

Your chief characteristic.

Your idea of happiness. To live in contact with those I love, with the beauties of nature, with a quantity of books and music, and to have, within easy distance, a French theater.
Your idea of misery. To be separated from Mama.

Your favourite colour and flower. I like them all and, for the flowers, I do not know.

If not yourself, who would you be? Since the question does not arise, I prefer not to answer it. All the same, I should very much have liked to be Pliny the Younger.
Where would you like to live? In the country of the Ideal, or, rather, of my ideal.

Your favourite prose authors. George Sand, Aug. Thierry.

Your favourite poets. Musset.

Your favourite painters and composers. Meissonier, Mozart, Gounod.

Your favourite heroes in real life. A mixture of Socrates, Pericles, Mahomet, Pliny the Younger and Augustin Thierry.
Your favourite heroines in real life. A woman of genius leading an ordinary life.

Your favourite heroes in fiction. Those of romance and poetry, those who are the expression of an ideal rather than an imitation of the real.
Your favourite heroines in fiction. Those who are more than women without ceasing to be womanly; everything that is tender, poetic, pure and in every way beautiful.
Your favourite food and drink.

Your favourite names.

Your pet aversion. People who do not feel what is good, who ignore the sweetness of affection.

What characters in history do you most dislike.

What is your present state of mind?

For what fault have you most toleration? To a life deprived of the works of genius.

Your favourite motto. One that cannot be summarized because its simplest form is what is beautiful, good, great in nature.

Your favourite virtue. *Toutes celles qui ne sont pas particulières à une secte, les universelles*

Your favourite qualities in man. *L'intelligence, le sens moral*

Your favourite qualities in woman. *La douceur, le naturel, l'intelligence*

Your favourite occupation. *, la lecture, la rêverie, les vers, l'histoire, le théâtre*

Your chief characteristic.

Your idea of happiness. *Vivre près de tous ceux que j'aime avec les charmes de la nature, une quantité de livres et de partitions et pas loin un théâtre français.*

Your idea of misery. *Être éloigné séparé de maman.*

Your favourite colour and flower. *Je les aime toutes, et pour les fleurs je ne sais pas*

If not yourself, who would you be? *N'ayant pas à me poser la question je préfère ne pas la résoudre, j'aurais cependant*

Where would you like to live? *bien aimé être Pline le Jeune.*
Au pays de l'idéal, ou plutôt de mon idéal.

Your favourite prose authors. *George Sand, Aug. Thierry.*

Your favourite poets. *Musset,*

Your favourite painters and composers. *Meissonnier. Mozart. Gounod*

Your favourite heroes in real life. *Un milieu entre Socrate, Périclès, Mahomet, Musset, Pl. le jeune, Aug. Thierry*

Your favourite heroines in real life. *Une femme de génie ayant l'existence d'une femme ordinaire*

Your favourite heroes in fiction. *Les héros romanesques poétiques, ceux qui sont un idéal, plutôt qu'un modèle*

Your favourite heroines in fiction. *Celles qui ne sont plus que des femmes seules sorties de leur sexe, tout ce qui est tendre, poétique, pur, beau dans tous les genres.*

Your favourite food and drink.

Your favourite names.

Your pet aversion. *Les gens qui ne sentent pas ce qui est bien, qui ignorent les douceurs de l'affection*

What characters in history do you most dislike.

What is your present state of mind?

For what fault have you most toleration? *Pour la vie privée des génies*

Your favourite motto. *Une qui ne peut pas se résumer parce que sa plus simple expression est ce qui a de beau, de bon, de grand dans la nature*

Your chief characteristic. A craving to be loved, or, to be more precise, to be caressed and spoiled rather than to be admired.

Your favourite qualities in a man. Feminine charm.

Your favourite qualities in a woman. A man's virtues, and frankness in friendship.

Your favourite qualities in friends. Tenderness – provided they possess a physical charm which makes their tenderness worth having.

Your biggest flaw. Lack of understanding: weakness of will.

Your favourite occupation. Loving.

Your idea of happiness. Not, I fear, a very elevated one. I really haven't the courage to say what it is, and if I did I should probably destroy it by the mere fact of putting it into word.

Your idea of misery. Never to have known my mother or my grandmother.

If not yourself, who would you be. Myself – as those whom I admire would like me to be.

Where would you like to live? One where certain things that I want would be realized – and where feelings of tenderness would always be reciprocate.

Your favourite colour and flower. Beauty lies not in colors but in their harmony. Hers – but apart from that, all.

Your favourite prose authors. At the moment, Anatole France and Pierre Loti.

Your favourite poets. Beaudelaire and Alfred de Vigny

Your favourite heroes in fiction. Hamlet.

Your favourite heroines in fiction. ~~Phedre~~ Berenice.

Your favourite composers. Beethoven, Wagner, Shuhmann.

Your favourite painters. Leonardo da Vinci, Rembrandt.

Your favourite heroes in real life. Monsieur Darlu, Monsieur Boutroux.

Your favourite heroine in history. Cleopatra.

Your favourite names. I only have one at a time.

Your pet aversion. My own worst qualities.

What characters in history do you most dislike. I am not sufficiently educated to say.

The military deed that you admire most. My own enlistment as a volunteer!

The reform that you appreciate.

What gift from nature would you like to have? Will power and irresistible charm.

How would you like to die? A better man than I am, and much beloved.

What is your present state of mind? Annoyance at having to think about myself in order to answer these questions.

For what fault have you most toleration? Those that I understand.

Your favourite motto. I prefer not to say, for fear it might bring me bad luck.

Marcel Proust par lui-même

Le principal trait de mon caractère.	le besoin d'être aimé et pour préciser plutôt le besoin d'être caressé et gâté bien plutôt que le besoin d'être admiré
La qualité que je désire chez un homme.	Des charmes féminins
La qualité que je préfère chez une femme. .	Des vertus d'homme et la franchise de la camaraderie
Ce que j'apprécie le plus chez mes amis . . .	D'être tendres pour moi si leur personne est assez exquise pour donner un grand prix à leur tendresse
Mon principal défaut	Ne pas savoir, ne pas pouvoir "vouloir"
Mon occupation préférée	Aimer
Mon rêve de bonheur	J'ai peur qu'il ne soit pas assez élevé, je n'ose pas le dire. Et j'ai peur de le détruire en le disant
Quel serait mon plus grand malheur. . . .	Ne pas avoir connu ma mère ni ma grand'mère
Ce que je voudrais être	Moi, comme les gens que j'admire me voudraient
Le pays où je désirerais vivre	Celui où certaines choses que je voudrais se réaliseraient comme par un enchantement — et où les tendresses seraient toujours partagées
La couleur que je préfère.	La beauté n'est pas dans les couleurs mais dans leur harmonie
La fleur que j'aime	La sienne — et après toutes
L'oiseau que je préfère	L'hirondelle
Mes auteurs favoris en prose	Aujourd'hui Anatole France et Pierre Loti
Mes poètes préférés.	Baudelaire et Alfred de Vigny
Mes héros dans la fiction	Hamlet
Mes héroïnes favorites dans la fiction. . .	Phèdre Bérénice
Mes compositeurs préférés.	Beethoven, Wagner, Schumann
Mes peintres favoris	Léonard de Vinci, Rembrandt
Mes héros dans la vie réelle	M. Darlu, M. Boutroux
Mes héroïnes dans l'histoire.	Cléopâtre
Mes noms favoris.	Je n'en ai qu'un à la fois
Ce que je déteste par-dessus tout.	Ce qu'il y a de mal en moi
Caractères historiques que je méprise le plus.	Je ne suis pas assez instruit
Le fait militaire que j'admire le plus . .	Mon volontariat !
La réforme que j'estime le plus	
Le don de la nature que je voudrais avoir . .	La volonté, et des séductions
Comment j'aimerais mourir.	Meilleur — et aimé
État présent de mon esprit.	L'ennui d'avoir pensé à moi pour répondre à toutes ces questions
Fautes qui m'inspirent le plus d'indulgence.	Celles que je comprends
Ma devise	J'aurais trop peur qu'elle ne me porte malheur

They answered...

The people who accepted to collaborate on this book
have answered to one of the two questionnaires Proust filled during his youth.
Questionnaire #1 corresponds to the questionnaire filled in 1886,
and questionnaire #2 corresponds to the one filled in 1890-91.

Isabelle Adjani

Your favourite virtue. Generosity.

Your favourite qualities in a man. Generous, unpredictable, funny, with a mysterious energy.

Your favourite qualities in a woman. Generous, spiritual, open-minded, and secretive.

Your favourite occupation. Today, to live everything that can be fully lived.

Your chief characteristic. To be torn when I am straightforward.

Your idea of happiness. Balance in everything with a few sparks of excess.

Your idea of misery. To be unbalanced in everything.

Your favourite colour and flower. The spectrum of white and all kinds of sweet-smelling white flowers.

If not yourself, who would you be? The most human.

Where would you like to live?   In the desert, next to the sea.

Your favourite prose authors. Stendhal, Chateaubriand, Proust, Duras, Sagan, Oscar Wilde, Freud, Cioran, Ryu Murakami, Kafka, Edith Wharton.

Your favourite poets. Arthur Rimbaud, Robert Frost, Baudelaire, René Char, Shakespeare, Francis Ponge, Emily Dickinson, Sylvia Plath.

Your favourite painters and composers. Leonardo da Vinci, Francis Bacon, Nicolas de Staël, Gustave Doré, Rembrandt, Caillebotte, George Romney, Burne Jones.

Your favourite heroes in real life. Alexandre Adler for intelligence, the resisting student in front of the tank in Tiananman Square, all those who are survivors.

Your favourite heroines in real life. All the survivors, the resistants, those of today and yesterday.

Your favourite heroes in fiction. They are related to music, the most powerful way to escape: Mozart, Beethoven, Bach, real composers, real geniuses, although to us, they seem to be part of the real in fiction + John Lennon, Serge Gainsbourg.

Your favourite heroines in fiction. Those who inspired me as a comedian – characters such as Racine's heroines.

Your favourite food and drink. Exotic, cosmopolitan, otherwise carrot purée (ethnic) with cumin and ginger juice (with spices).

Your favourite names. Brocéliande, Knight, Lynx, Wallaby, Byron, Staël, Pamina, Mélisande, for the kids I shall have in another life.

Your pet aversion. Stupidity and ignorance, a two-headed monster.

What characters in history do you most dislike.   Those responsible for crimes against humanity, both passively and actively.

What is your present state of mind? Free to live my passions.

For what fault have you most toleration? Exaggeration when it is a matter of excess, but not when it contains sadistic or cruel intentions.

Your favourite motto. Suffering is needless unless you are in love.

Your favourite virtue.

Your favourite qualities in a man.

Your favourite qualities in a woman.

Your favourite occupation.

Your chief characteristic.

Your idea of happiness.

Your idea of misery.

Your favourite colour and flower.

If not yourself, who would you be?

Where would you like to live?

Your favourite prose authors.

Your favourite poets.

Your favourite painters and composers.

Your favourite heroes in real life.

Your favourite heroines in real life.

Your favourite heroes in fiction.

Your favourite heroines in fiction.

Your favourite food and drink.

Your favourite names.

Your pet aversion.

What characters in history do you most dislike.

What is your present state of mind?

For what fault have you most toleration?

Your favourite motto.

Your favourite virtue. **Forgiveness**

Your favourite qualities in a man. PASSION — Humour, intelligence Loving communicative

Your favourite qualities in a woman. PASSION - Humour - intelligence - Loving Communicative. Forgiveness -

Your favourite occupation. Motherhood, Director

Your chief characteristic. **Honesty —**

Your idea of happiness. HAVING LOVE - Be constant -

Your idea of misery. LIVING IN The United States with George W Bush As President for Another 4 years —.

Your favourite colour and flower. Blue- Gardenia, Violet, Sunflowers

If not yourself, who would you be? My Daughter Zoe-

Where would you like to live? Paris —FRANCE —

Your favourite prose authors. Anne Sexton— Rimbaud, patti smith, Joni Mitchell

Your favourite poets. My mother Manoi; Augnette a great poet

Your favourite painters and composers. MAX Ernst, Van Gough, John Lennon — Jonatha Elias — Graham Dean— Joni mitchell

Your favourite heroes in real life. MARTIN Luther King—

Your favourite heroines in real life. Joni Mitchell John AND Yoko ono Lennon

Your favourite heroes in fiction. The Cowardly Lion — in The Wizard of oz

Your favourite heroines in fiction. Anna Karenina, Dorthy — in The Wizard of oz —

Your favourite food and drink. Champagne (Bellini's) Caviar

Your favourite names. Zoe- Gabriel — Danielle Coco

Your pet aversion. **RATS**

What characters in history do you most dislike. Hitler —

What is your present state of mind? Happy- Calm - inspired In Love —

For what fault have you most toleration? Tardiness —

Your favourite motto. WAR IS OVER IF YOU WANT it! (John Lennon) Give Peace A Chance!

Brigitte Bardot

Your chief characteristic. Absolutism.

Your favourite qualities in a man. To be a bit more than a woman.

Your favourite qualities in a woman. The beauty of the heart.

Your favourite qualities in friends. Their availability.

Your biggest flaw. Intrinsic intransigence.

Your favourite occupation. Dreaming.

Your idea of happiness. A vegetarian world, believing in what Tolstoy said: "As long as there are slaughterhouses there will be battlefields."

Your idea of misery. To lose my fight for the protection of animals.

If not yourself, who would you be? A Fairy.

Where would you like to live?   On the planet of flowers.

Your favourite colour and flower. Orange. Marguerite (Daisy).

Your favourite prose authors. Yourcenar, St Exupery.

Your favourite poets Cros ."Bilon" my dad.

Your favourite heroes in fiction. The beast in *The Beauty and the Beast*.

Your favourite heroines in fiction. Snow White.

Your favourite composers. Beethoven, Chopin, Weber.

Your favourite painters. Le Douanier Rousseau, Botticelli.

Your favourite heroes in real life. Leonardo da Vinci.

Your favourite heroine in history. Joan of Arc.

Your favourite names. Emma, Linea.

Your pet aversion. Mediocrity.

What characters in history do you most dislike. Stalin's ideology.

The military deed that you admire most. Peace.

The reform that you appreciate. When God created woman.

What gift from nature would you like to have? To work miracles.

How would you like to die? Of Love!

What is your present state of mind? Skeptical.

For what fault have you most toleration. Regrets.

Your favourite motto. Noise does not do you good. To do good makes no noise.

Your favourite virtue.

Your favourite qualities in a man.

Your favourite qualities in a woman.

Your favourite occupation.

Your chief characteristic.

Your idea of happiness.

Your idea of misery.

Your favourite colour and flower.

If not yourself, who would you be?

Where would you like to live?

Your favourite prose authors.

Your favourite poets.

Your favourite painters and composers.

Your favourite heroes in real life.

Your favourite heroines in real life.

Your favourite heroes in fiction.

Your favourite heroines in fiction.

Your favourite food and drink.

Your favourite names.

Your pet aversion.

What characters in history do you most dislike.

What is your present state of mind?

For what fault have you most toleration?

Your favourite motto.

Your favourite virtue. Humility

Your favourite qualities in a man. Integrity, Depth, intelligence

Your favourite qualities in a woman. Courage, understanding, intelligence, Friendship

Your favourite occupation. Cinema

Your chief characteristic. Faith

Your idea of happiness. Harmony

Your idea of misery. Sickness, war

Your favourite colour and flower. Rainbow, Orchids

If not yourself, who would you be? A Fairy

Where would you like to live? New York, Paris

Your favourite prose authors. Gabriel Garcia Márquez, Stefan Zweig, Maria Corelli, Nietzsche, Jane Austin, Nina Berberova.

Your favourite poets. Kahlil Gibran, Pablo Neruda, Fernando Pessoa.

Your favourite painters and composers. Dante Rossetti, Gustave Klimt, Marcel Duchamp, Edward Burne-Jones, Tamara de Lempicka.

Your favourite heroes in real life. the Pope, Nelson Mandela, Gandhi, Abbé Pierre, Jesus Christ

Your favourite heroines in real life. The Virgin Mary, Audrey Hepburn, Mother Theresa, Lou Salomé.

Your favourite heroes in fiction. King Arthur, Merlin, Rhett Butler.

Your favourite heroines in fiction. Sheherazade, Anna Karenina, Joan of Arc, Madame de Staël.

Your favourite food and drink. Pasta, Salads, Turkey, earl grey Tea

Your favourite names. Starlite, Anastasia

Your pet aversion. Lack of Freedom

What characters in history do you most dislike. Ben Laden, Hitler.

What is your present state of mind? Constructive

For what fault have you most toleration? Impatience

Your favourite motto. Love one Another

Alain de Botton

Alain de Botton

Your chief characteristic. A desire to understand the world.

Your favourite qualities in a man. An absence of machismo.

Your favourite qualities in a woman. An absence of hysteria.

Your favourite qualities in friends. The capacity to be honest their problems

Your biggest flaw. Constant anxiety.

Your favourite occupation. Writing..

Your idea of happiness. Writing well.

Your idea of misery. Writing badly.

If not yourself, who would you be? Stendhal

Where would you like to live? London, but with sunshine.

Your favourite colour and flower. Celadon Daffodils

Your favourite prose authors. Montaigne, Roland Barthes, Milan Kundera.

Your favourite poets Baudelaire Larkin

Your favourite heroes in fiction. Young Werther

Your favourite heroines in fiction. Madame Bovary

Your favourite composers. Bach

Your favourite painters. Købke, Hammershøi

Your favourite heroes in real life. Vaclav Havel

Your favourite heroine in history. Joan of Arc

Your favourite names. Eloise, Samuel

Your pet aversion. Cruelty

What characters in history do you most dislike. Fascists

The military deed that you admire most. Sacrifice for a good cause.

The reform that you appreciate. Democracy

What gift from nature would you like to have? Calm

How would you like to die? Late in life.

What is your present state of mind? Bored by this.

For what fault have you most toleration. Despair

Your favourite motto. 'What need is there to weep over parts of life? The whole of it calls for tears.' Seneca _daniel boulud_

Daniel Boulud

Your favourite virtue. Loyalty

Your favourite qualities in a man. Trustworthiness

Your favourite qualities in a woman. intelligence & care

Your favourite occupation. Still searching

Your chief characteristic.

Your idea of happiness. not working

Your idea of misery. being stuck in traffic

Your favourite colour and flower. Red Ferrari & White Orchid

If not yourself, who would you be? myself at 16 again.

Where would you like to live? Provence

Your favourite prose authors. Guy de Maupassant

Your favourite poets.

Your favourite painters and composers. Picasso & Sting

Your favourite heroes in real life. Lafayette

Your favourite heroines in real life. Marie Curie

Your favourite heroes in fiction. Captain Picard "Star Treck"

Your favourite heroines in fiction. Athena

Your favourite food and drink. Truffles Black or White. Red wine chateauneuf du Pape

Your favourite names. Aston Martin

Your pet aversion. Snake

What characters in history do you most dislike. Hitler

What is your present state of mind? Busy, but happily so!

For what fault have you most toleration? Tardiness

Your favourite motto. if you can afford it. "Eat it or Drink it"

Anh Duong

Your chief characteristic. *Questionning*

Your favourite qualities in a man. *Attention*

Your favourite qualities in a woman. *confidence*

Your favourite qualities in friends. *Faithful, sense of humor, cultivated*

Your biggest flaw. *To doubt*

Your favourite occupation. *To love and being loved*

Your idea of happiness. *Enjoying what I have*

Your idea of misery. *Regretting the past, worrying about the future*

If not yourself, who would you be? *My true self*

Where would you like to live?

Your favourite colour and flower. *Flesh Peony*

Your favourite prose authors. *Cioran*

Your favourite poets *My lovers*

Your favourite heroes in fiction. *Le petit prince*

Your favourite heroines in fiction. *I can't think of one who didn't have a tragic ending to pay for her sins*

Your favourite composers. *Malher, Bach, Georges Delerue*

Your favourite painters. *Manet, Velasquez, and myself Twombly*

Your favourite heroes in real life. *Gandhi*

Your favourite heroine in history. *Cleopatra*

Your favourite names. *Any flowers names*

Your pet aversion. *Cowardness*

What characters in history do you most dislike. *Any dictator*

The military deed that you admire most. *military and admire don't go together*

The reform that you appreciate.

What gift from nature would you like to have?

How would you like to die?

What is your present state of mind?

For what fault have you most toleration. *The ones I don't have*

Your favourite motto. *What would you do if you knew you couldn't fail?*

Diane von Furstenberg

Diane von Furstenberg

Your favourite virtue. Intelligence

Your favourite qualities in a man. strength

Your favourite qualities in a woman. loyalty

Your favourite occupation. reading

Your chief characteristic.

Your idea of happiness. To be free

Your idea of misery. To loose freedom

Your favourite colour and flower. all colors all flowers

If not yourself, who would you be? a tree

Where would you like to live? at home

Your favourite prose authors. PUIG – GRASS – Hans Fallada – Oscar Wilde – Tolstoi

Your favourite poets. KEATS – RIMBAUD. BAUDELAIRE

Your favourite painters and composers. Bach GOYA

Your favourite heroes in real life. Leonardo da Vinci –

Your favourite heroines in real life. Cleopatra

Your favourite heroes in fiction. DON QUIXOTTE

Your favourite heroines in fiction. All mothers

Your favourite food and drink. DON QUIXOTTE

Your favourite names. Alexandra & Tatiana

Your pet aversion. ?

What characters in history do you most dislike. the weak ones.

What is your present state of mind? Personally peaceful – concerned about our planet.

For what fault have you most toleration? Fear is not an apt option

Your favourite motto.

Serge Lutens

Serge Lutens

Your favourite virtue. Modesty – for centuries, people were having "modesty baths".

Your favourite qualities in a man. Kindness, generosity…

Your favourite qualities in a woman. Intuition, spirit…

Your favourite occupation. It indeed overruns me. It is not a choice: to admire, to appreciate,
to discover, to work…

Your chief characteristic. I'm a dreamer!

Your idea of happiness. Its name did it great wrong.

Your idea of misery. To lose taste.

Your favourite colour and flower. White to inscribe black on it. My favourite flower for its name
and its perfume: rose.

If not yourself, who would you be? One of the Queen's pageboys.

Where would you like to live? In my house, in Marrakech.

Your favourite prose authors. Jean Genet, Marcel Proust, Charles Dodgson (Lewis Carroll),
Louis-Ferdinand Céline, Gaston Bachelard.

Your favourite poets. The ones I read: Charles Baudelaire, Jean Genet, Rainer Maria Rilke.

Your favourite painters and composers. Bach, Stravinsky, Gershwin, Strauss… The Lascaux wall paint-
ings, Michel-Ange, Rembrandt, Raphaël, Vélasquez, Le Gréco, Bonnard, Picasso, Cézanne, Matisse…

Your favourite heroes in real life. Rimbaud because he disappears, Mishima with his "Sepuku".
In fact, all the ones who want to go further, the ones who understand they can go further.

Your favourite heroines in real life. The ones who reveal themselves with dignity: Joan of Arc during
her trial, Marie-Antoinette when her son, the dauphin, is taken from her.

Your favourite heroes in fiction. Good God, the Devil.

Your favourite heroines in fiction. The Queen of the Night in *The Magic Flute* and Garance in
Marcel Carné's *Children of Paradise*.

Your favourite food and drink. The delicious simplicity, the very fresh sparkling water.

Your favourite names. Pierre, Paul, Matthieu, Jean, Gabriel, Luc, David, Maximilien, Suleyman,
Abdelkrim, Blanche, Souha, Esther, Rachel, Marthe, Rose.

Your pet aversion. Pretention, stupidity which can echo some ways of intelligence.
All can be obstacles to sensibility.

What characters in history do you most dislike. The masters of the world who talk, act in the name of the good,
of the bad, of moral, of reason. People are however composed of instants and I like Louis XIV when he dances.

What is your present state of mind? One more Proust questionnaire!

For what fault have you most toleration? In fact, for all when they're justified, i.e. they are well-done.
A kind of perfect crime, as an artist.

Your favourite motto. I don't really have one. I'll conclude: such is our "Denise"
[motto is "Devise" in French]. Denise is my mother's name.

Richard Meier

Your favourite virtue. Accountability

Your favourite qualities in a man. Veraciousness, intelligence, openness

Your favourite qualities in a woman. Intelligence, candidness, fastidiousness, responsible

Your favourite occupation. Architecture

Your chief characteristic.

Your idea of happiness. Working late

Your idea of misery. Waiting in an airport for an airplane to take off that is continually delayed

Your favourite colour and flower. White calla lily

If not yourself, who would you be? Picasso

Where would you like to live? In New York City

Your favourite prose authors. Franz Kafka, Elie Wiesel, Robert Hughes, Arthur A. Cohen

Your favourite poets.

Your favourite painters and composers. De Kooning, Picasso, Matisse, Schiele, Cézanne. Beethoven, Brahms & Mahler and Barnett Newman

Your favourite heroes in real life. Nelson Mandela, Michaelangelo, John F. Kennedy

Your favourite heroines in real life.

Your favourite heroes in fiction. Howard Roark

Your favourite heroines in fiction. Anna Karenina

Your favourite food and drink. Sashimi & wine

Your favourite names. Ana and Joseph

Your pet aversion. Being stuck in an airplane that is circling the airport waiting for permission to land.

What characters in history do you most dislike. All Dictators

What is your present state of mind? Clear and optimistic

For what fault have you most toleration? Inconsistency

Your favourite motto.

Your chief characteristic.

Your favourite qualities in a man.

Your favourite qualities in a woman.

Your favourite qualities in friends.

Your biggest flaw.

Your favourite occupation.

Your idea of happiness.

Your idea of misery.

If not yourself, who would you be?

Where would you like to live?

Your favourite colour and flower.

Your favourite prose authors.

Your favourite poets   .

Your favourite heroes in fiction.

Your favourite heroines in fiction.

Your favourite composers.

Your favourite painters.

Your favourite heroes in real life.

Your favourite heroine in history.

Your favourite names.

Your pet aversion.

What characters in history do you most dislike.

The military deed that you admire most.

The reform that you appreciate.

What gift from nature would you like to have?

How would you like to die?

What is your present state of mind?

For what fault have you most toleration.

Your favourite motto.

Your chief characteristic. Kindness and simplicity.

Your favourite qualities in a man. Frankness and honesty.

Your favourite qualities in a woman. Simplicity, kindness and gentleness.

Your favourite qualities in friends. That they don't forget from where they come.

Your biggest flaw. Stubborn, impatient.

Your favourite occupation. Basketball.

Your idea of happiness. Winning NBA titles, having a happy family and kids.

Your idea of misery. Not having a good family or having my friends changed.

If not yourself, who would you be? A man who enjoys modest success.

Where would you like to live?   The United States.

Your favourite colour and flower. Red. Tulips.

Your favourite prose authors. Antoine de St. Exupéry.

Your favourite poets   .

Your favourite heroes in fiction. Spiderman.

Your favourite heroines in fiction. Catwoman and Sydney Bristow (*Alias*).

Your favourite composers. 50 Cent, Jay-Z.

Your favourite painters. Justin Bua.

Your favourite heroes in real life. Michael Jordan.

Your favourite heroine in history. Joan of Arc.

Your favourite names. Emma, Linea.

Your pet aversion. Hypocrisy.

What characters in history do you most dislike. Hitler.

The military deed that you admire most. The Normandy landings.

The reform that you appreciate. I have a dream by Martin Luther King.

What gift from nature would you like to have? To fly as a bird.

How would you like to die? Naturally, without suffering.

What is your present state of mind? Positive, happy, fulfilled.

For what fault have you most toleration. Clumsiness and incomprehension.

Your favourite motto. Always try to find a way to be positive.

Andrée Putman

Andrée Putman

Your favourite virtue. Imagination.

Your favourite qualities in a man. Independence.

Your favourite qualities in a woman. Independence.

Your favourite occupation. Conversation.

Your chief characteristic. Will.

Your idea of happiness. The light.

Your idea of misery. To be in a rut.

Your favourite colour and flower. Blacks and poppies.

If not yourself, who would you be? Saint Teresa of Avila.

Where would you like to live? Where I live, in the 6th arrondissement of Paris.

Your favourite prose authors. Beckett, Cioran, Claude Simon, Raymond Carver, Marguerite Duras.

Your favourite poets. Baudelaire, René Char.

Your favourite painters and composers. Louise Bourgeois, Paul Klee, Bram vam Velze, Alban Berg.

Your favourite heroes in real life. Jean Moulin.

Your favourite heroines in real life. Simone Veil, Françoise Dolto.

Your favourite heroes in fiction. Achille.

Your favourite heroines in fiction. Marguerite Duras, the heroine of her own books.

Your favourite food and drink. Sole meunière and Grand Bordeaux.

Your favourite names. Olivia, Grazia, Olympia.

Your pet aversion. The conservative mind.

What characters in history do you most dislike. The commandant Henry, who forged a paper to accuse Captain Dreyfus.

What is your present state of mind? The invention of the future.

For what fault have you most toleration? Excesses.

Your favourite motto. Always ready.

Lee Radziwill (signature)

Lee Radziwill

Your favourite virtue. COMPASSION

Your favourite qualities in a man. HUMOUR, un peu coureur

Your favourite qualities in a woman. Warmth, HUMOUR

Your favourite occupation. Painting Botanicals & Watching Ballet.

Your chief characteristic. Laziness

Your idea of happiness. Being on the SEA and In the Sea

Your idea of misery. RAIN

Your favourite colour and flower. Fuchsia Peonies

If not yourself, who would you be? no IDEA

Where would you like to live? where I live, Paris

Your favourite prose authors. TRUMAN CAPOTE " OTHER VOICES, OTHER Rooms "

Your favourite poets. BYRON

Your favourite painters and composers. Vuillard), Rodgers & HART

Your favourite heroes in real life. Vuillard), Rodgers & HART John KERRY

Your favourite heroines in real life. Any woman who has really suffered).

Your favourite heroes in fiction. JAmes BonD

Your favourite heroines in fiction. SCARLETT O'HARA

Your favourite food and drink. Pommes Puree & Saucisson Chaud

Your favourite names. Zoë, ZELDA & Hamilton

Your pet aversion. When People are late

What characters in history do you most dislike. Dictators, Stalin, Hitler etc.

What is your present state of mind? It changes

For what fault have you most toleration? SHYNESS

Your favourite motto. " There is nothing to fear but
fear itself".
President Franklin Roosevelt

Your favourite virtue.

Your favourite qualities in a man.

Your favourite qualities in a woman.

Your favourite occupation.

Your chief characteristic.

Your idea of happiness.

Your idea of misery.

Your favourite colour and flower.

If not yourself, who would you be?

Where would you like to live?

Your favourite prose authors.

Your favourite poets.

Your favourite painters and composers.

Your favourite heroes in real life.

Your favourite heroines in real life.

Your favourite heroes in fiction.

Your favourite heroines in fiction.

Your favourite food and drink.

Your favourite names.

Your pet aversion.

What characters in history do you most dislike.

What is your present state of mind?

For what fault have you most toleration?

Your favourite motto.

Your favourite virtue. Diplomacy.

Your favourite qualities in a man. Responsibility and humor.

Your favourite qualities in a woman. Femininity and the willingness to listen to other people.

Your favourite occupation. Working, swimming, and embroidery.

Your chief characteristic. Tenacity.

Your idea of happiness. When my son tells me: "Mommy, I love you."

Your idea of misery. Not to have friends.

Your favourite colour and flower. All colors, waterlily.

If not yourself, who would you be? ?

Where would you like to live? In my home only.

Your favourite prose authors. Sacha Guitry, Labiche, Beaumarchais.

Your favourite poets. Omar Khayyam, Ronsard.

Your favourite painters and composers. Rembrandt, Renoir, Francis Bacon, Offenbach, Sidney Bechet, Jean-Michel Jarre.

Your favourite heroes in real life. Louis Pasteur, Moshe Dayan, Pr René Frydman.

Your favourite heroines in real life. Hillary Clinton, Marie Curie.

Your favourite heroes in fiction. Robin Hood, Cinderella's Prince Charming, Inspector Derrick.

Your favourite heroines in fiction. Barbie, Miss Marple.

Your favourite food and drink. The 7-hours-cooked leg of lamb, Château Malmaison.

Your favourite names. Noémie, Alice, Eve, Olivia.

Your pet aversion. Hunger.

What characters in history do you most dislike. Attila.

What is your present state of mind? Live and let live.

For what fault have you most toleration? Stupidity.

Your favourite motto. Tomorrow's another day.

Luc Sante

Luc Sante

Your favourite virtue. Charity

Your favourite qualities in a man. humor, curiosity, skepticism, self-doubt

Your favourite qualities in a woman. humor, curiosity, skepticism, mutability

Your favourite occupation, professional namer
(giving names to, e.g., cars, drugs, asteroids)

Your chief characteristic.

Your idea of happiness. Working well, domestic harmony prevailing and all debts paid, with
the occasional chance to travel

Your idea of misery. Existing under the rule of a superior --
employer or likewise

Your favourite colour and flower. forest green; the dahlia

If not yourself, who would you be? an international jewel thief

Where would you like to live? the mountains (these or other) in the summer,
New Orleans in the winter

Your favourite prose authors. Melville, Flaubert, Stephen Crane, Walter Benjamin

Your favourite poets.

Your favourite painters and composers. Brueghel, Goya, Manet; Wm. Byrd, Thomas Tallis, Bach

Your favourite heroes in real life. Crazy Horse, Arthur Cravan, Louis Armstrong

Your favourite heroines in real life. Louise Michel, Bessie Smith, Valerie Solanas

Your favourite heroes in fiction. Huckleberry Finn, Svejk, Cosmo Piovasco di Rondò

Your favourite heroines in fiction. Moll Flanders, Nadja, Irma Vep

Your favourite food and drink. oysters + champagne

Your favourite names. Raphael, Indio; Olive, Mitsouko

Your pet aversion. patriotism

What characters in history do you most dislike. St. Paul, Oliver Cromwell, Leopold II,
J. Edgar Hoover

What is your present state of mind? anxious, watchful

For what fault have you most toleration? indolence

Your favourite motto. I can't go on, I'll go on

Bernar Venet (signature)

Bernar Venet

Your chief characteristic. To doubt all the values that I have been taught.

Your favourite qualities in a man. To be daring

Your favourite qualities in a woman. To have them all

Your favourite qualities in friends. An ability to surprise me, and a respect for our differences.

Your biggest flaw. Impatience.

Your favourite occupation. to make Art, to look at art, to acquire art.

Your idea of happiness. — A lack of imagination, the lack of consciousness of the misery that surrounds us.

Your idea of misery. Not to be respected.

If not yourself, who would you be? A better artist

Where would you like to live? In New York, in Le Roy and once in a while in Paris.

Your favourite colour and flower. White when not black. White tulips when offered

Your favourite prose authors. All great philosophers

Your favourite poets All those whose poetry I don't yet fully understand

Your favourite heroes in fiction When I was 8 years old : Tarzan

Your favourite heroines in fiction. Liz and Beth

Your favourite composers. John Cage, particularly "Silence"

Your favourite painters. Malevitch, Ryman, Don Judd, Ad Reinhardt.

Your favourite heroes in real life. Diogène, Kurt Gödel, A. Solzhenitsyn.

Your favourite heroine in history. My mother

Your favourite names. Saskia, Bérénice, Esther, Zarathoustra

Your pet aversion. People who overestimate the pleasure of food.

What characters in history do you most dislike. The author of Mein Kampf

The military deed that you admire most. The Liberation of Paris in 1944

The reform that you appreciate. The next reform that will reform the reforms

What gift from nature would you like to have? A memory of the future

How would you like to die? Thinking as I do today, that it's not a big deal.

What is your present state of mind? Better than ever,

For what fault have you most toleration. Inexposure to culture.

Your favourite motto. Que m'importe ce qui n'importe qu'à moi.

The questionnaire game...

Questionnaire #1 and questionnaire #2
are alternatively reproduced in the following pages.

Your favourite virtue. _____

Your favourite qualities in a man. _____

Your favourite qualities in a woman. _____

Your favourite occupation. _____

Your chief characteristic. _____

Your idea of happiness. _____

Your idea of misery. _____

Your favourite colour and flower. _____

If not yourself, who would you be? _____

Where would you like to live? _____

Your favourite prose authors. _____

Your favourite poets. _____

Your favourite painters and composers. _____

Your favourite heroes in real life. _____

Your favourite heroines in real life. _____

Your favourite heroes in fiction. _____

Your favourite heroines in fiction. _____

Your favourite food and drink. _____

Your favourite names. _____

Your pet aversion. _____

What characters in History do you most dislike. _____

What is your present state of mind? _____

For what fault have you most toleration? _____

Your favourite motto. _____

Your favourite virtue. _____

Your favourite qualities in a man. _____

Your favourite qualities in a woman. _____

Your favourite occupation. _____

Your chief characteristic. _____

Your idea of happiness. _____

Your idea of misery. _____

Your favourite colour and flower. _____

If not yourself, who would you be? _____

Where would you like to live? _____

Your favourite prose authors. _____

Your favourite poets. _____

Your favourite painters and composers. _____

Your favourite heroes in real life. _____

Your favourite heroines in real life. _____

Your favourite heroes in fiction. _____

Your favourite heroines in fiction. _____

Your favourite food and drink. _____

Your favourite names. _____

Your pet aversion. _____

What characters in History do you most dislike. _____

What is your present state of mind? _____

For what fault have you most toleration? _____

Your favourite motto. _____

Your chief characteristic. _____

Your favourite qualities in a man. _____

Your favourite qualities in a woman. _____

Your favourite qualities in friends. _____

Your biggest flaw. _____

Your favourite occupation. _____

Your idea of happiness. _____

Your idea of misery. _____

If not yourself, who would you be? _____

Where would you like to live? _____

Your favourite colour and flower. _____

Your favourite prose authors. _____

Your favourite poets. _____

Your favourite heroes in fiction. _____

Your favourite heroines in fiction. _____

Your favourite composers. _____

Your favourite painters. _____

Your favourite heroes in real life. _____

Your favourite heroine in history. _____

Your favourite names. _____

Your pet aversion. _____

What characters in history do you most dislike. _____

The military deed that you admire most. _____

The reform that you appreciate. _____

What gift from nature would you like to have? _____

How would you like to die? _____

What is your present state of mind? _____

For what fault have you most toleration? _____

Your favourite motto. _____

Your chief characteristic. _____

Your favourite qualities in a man. _____

Your favourite qualities in a woman. _____

Your favourite qualities in friends. _____

Your biggest flaw. _____

Your favourite occupation. _____

Your idea of happiness. _____

Your idea of misery. _____

If not yourself, who would you be? _____

Where would you like to live? _____

Your favourite colour and flower. _____

Your favourite prose authors. _____

Your favourite poets. _____

Your favourite heroes in fiction. _____

Your favourite heroines in fiction. _____

Your favourite composers. _____

Your favourite painters. _____

Your favourite heroes in real life. _____

Your favourite heroine in history. _____

Your favourite names. _____

Your pet aversion. _____

What characters in history do you most dislike. _____

The military deed that you admire most. _____

The reform that you appreciate. _____

What gift from nature would you like to have? _____

How would you like to die? _____

What is your present state of mind? _____

For what fault have you most toleration? _____

Your favourite motto. _____

Your favourite virtue. _____

Your favourite qualities in a man. _____

Your favourite qualities in a woman. _____

Your favourite occupation. _____

Your chief characteristic. _____

Your idea of happiness. _____

Your idea of misery. _____

Your favourite colour and flower. _____

If not yourself, who would you be? _____

Where would you like to live? _____

Your favourite prose authors. _____

Your favourite poets. _____

Your favourite painters and composers. _____

Your favourite heroes in real life. _____

Your favourite heroines in real life. _____

Your favourite heroes in fiction. _____

Your favourite heroines in fiction. _____

Your favourite food and drink. _____

Your favourite names. _____

Your pet aversion. _____

What characters in History do you most dislike. _____

What is your present state of mind? _____

For what fault have you most toleration? _____

Your favourite motto. _____

Your favourite virtue. _____

Your favourite qualities in a man. _____

Your favourite qualities in a woman. _____

Your favourite occupation. _____

Your chief characteristic. _____

Your idea of happiness. _____

Your idea of misery. _____

Your favourite colour and flower. _____

If not yourself, who would you be? _____

Where would you like to live? _____

Your favourite prose authors. _____

Your favourite poets. _____

Your favourite painters and composers. _____

Your favourite heroes in real life. _____

Your favourite heroines in real life. _____

Your favourite heroes in fiction. _____

Your favourite heroines in fiction. _____

Your favourite food and drink. _____

Your favourite names. _____

Your pet aversion. _____

What characters in History do you most dislike. _____

What is your present state of mind? _____

For what fault have you most toleration? _____

Your favourite motto. _____

Your chief characteristic. _____

Your favourite qualities in a man. _____

Your favourite qualities in a woman. _____

Your favourite qualities in friends. _____

Your biggest flaw. _____

Your favourite occupation. _____

Your idea of happiness. _____

Your idea of misery. _____

If not yourself, who would you be? _____

Where would you like to live? _____

Your favourite colour and flower. _____

Your favourite prose authors. _____

Your favourite poets. _____

Your favourite heroes in fiction. _____

Your favourite heroines in fiction. _____

Your favourite composers. _____

Your favourite painters. _____

Your favourite heroes in real life. _____

Your favourite heroine in history. _____

Your favourite names. _____

Your pet aversion. _____

What characters in history do you most dislike. _____

The military deed that you admire most. _____

The reform that you appreciate. _____

What gift from nature would you like to have? _____

How would you like to die? _____

What is your present state of mind? _____

For what fault have you most toleration? _____

Your favourite motto. _____

questionnaire #2

Your chief characteristic. _____

Your favourite qualities in a man. _____

Your favourite qualities in a woman. _____

Your favourite qualities in friends. _____

Your biggest flaw. _____

Your favourite occupation. _____

Your idea of happiness. _____

Your idea of misery. _____

If not yourself, who would you be? _____

Where would you like to live? _____

Your favourite colour and flower. _____

Your favourite prose authors. _____

Your favourite poets. _____

Your favourite heroes in fiction. _____

Your favourite heroines in fiction. _____

Your favourite composers. _____

Your favourite painters. _____

Your favourite heroes in real life. _____

Your favourite heroine in history. _____

Your favourite names. _____

Your pet aversion. _____

What characters in history do you most dislike. _____

The military deed that you admire most. _____

The reform that you appreciate. _____

What gift from nature would you like to have? _____

How would you like to die? _____

What is your present state of mind? _____

For what fault have you most toleration? _____

Your favourite motto. _____

Your favourite virtue. _____

Your favourite qualities in a man. _____

Your favourite qualities in a woman. _____

Your favourite occupation. _____

Your chief characteristic. _____

Your idea of happiness. _____

Your idea of misery. _____

Your favourite colour and flower. _____

If not yourself, who would you be? _____

Where would you like to live? _____

Your favourite prose authors. _____

Your favourite poets. _____

Your favourite painters and composers. _____

Your favourite heroes in real life. _____

Your favourite heroines in real life. _____

Your favourite heroes in fiction. _____

Your favourite heroines in fiction. _____

Your favourite food and drink. _____

Your favourite names. _____

Your pet aversion. _____

What characters in History do you most dislike. _____

What is your present state of mind? _____

For what fault have you most toleration? _____

Your favourite motto. _____

65

Your favourite virtue. _____

Your favourite qualities in a man. _____

Your favourite qualities in a woman. _____

Your favourite occupation. _____

Your chief characteristic. _____

Your idea of happiness. _____

Your idea of misery. _____

Your favourite colour and flower. _____

If not yourself, who would you be? _____

Where would you like to live? _____

Your favourite prose authors. _____

Your favourite poets. _____

Your favourite painters and composers. _____

Your favourite heroes in real life. _____

Your favourite heroines in real life. _____

Your favourite heroes in fiction. _____

Your favourite heroines in fiction. _____

Your favourite food and drink. _____

Your favourite names. _____

Your pet aversion. _____

What characters in History do you most dislike. _____

What is your present state of mind? _____

For what fault have you most toleration? _____

Your favourite motto. _____

Your chief characteristic. _____

Your favourite qualities in a man. _____

Your favourite qualities in a woman. _____

Your favourite qualities in friends. _____

Your biggest flaw. _____

Your favourite occupation. _____

Your idea of happiness. _____

Your idea of misery. _____

If not yourself, who would you be? _____

Where would you like to live? _____

Your favourite colour and flower. _____

Your favourite prose authors. _____

Your favourite poets. _____

Your favourite heroes in fiction. _____

Your favourite heroines in fiction. _____

Your favourite composers. _____

Your favourite painters. _____

Your favourite heroes in real life. _____

Your favourite heroine in history. _____

Your favourite names. _____

Your pet aversion. _____

What characters in history do you most dislike. _____

The military deed that you admire most. _____

The reform that you appreciate. _____

What gift from nature would you like to have? _____

How would you like to die? _____

What is your present state of mind? _____

For what fault have you most toleration? _____

Your favourite motto. _____

Your chief characteristic. _____

Your favourite qualities in a man. _____

Your favourite qualities in a woman. _____

Your favourite qualities in friends. _____

Your biggest flaw. _____

Your favourite occupation. _____

Your idea of happiness. _____

Your idea of misery. _____

If not yourself, who would you be? _____

Where would you like to live? _____

Your favourite colour and flower. _____

Your favourite prose authors. _____

Your favourite poets. _____

Your favourite heroes in fiction. _____

Your favourite heroines in fiction. _____

Your favourite composers. _____

Your favourite painters. _____

Your favourite heroes in real life. _____

Your favourite heroine in history. _____

Your favourite names. _____

Your pet aversion. _____

What characters in history do you most dislike. _____

The military deed that you admire most. _____

The reform that you appreciate. _____

What gift from nature would you like to have? _____

How would you like to die? _____

What is your present state of mind? _____

For what fault have you most toleration? _____

Your favourite motto. _____

Your favourite virtue. _____

Your favourite qualities in a man. _____

Your favourite qualities in a woman. _____

Your favourite occupation. _____

Your chief characteristic. _____

Your idea of happiness. _____

Your idea of misery. _____

Your favourite colour and flower. _____

If not yourself, who would you be? _____

Where would you like to live? _____

Your favourite prose authors. _____

Your favourite poets. _____

Your favourite painters and composers. _____

Your favourite heroes in real life. _____

Your favourite heroines in real life. _____

Your favourite heroes in fiction. _____

Your favourite heroines in fiction. _____

Your favourite food and drink. _____

Your favourite names. _____

Your pet aversion. _____

What characters in History do you most dislike. _____

What is your present state of mind? _____

For what fault have you most toleration? _____

Your favourite motto. _____

Your favourite virtue. _____

Your favourite qualities in a man. _____

Your favourite qualities in a woman. _____

Your favourite occupation. _____

Your chief characteristic. _____

Your idea of happiness. _____

Your idea of misery. _____

Your favourite colour and flower. _____

If not yourself, who would you be? _____

Where would you like to live? _____

Your favourite prose authors. _____

Your favourite poets. _____

Your favourite painters and composers. _____

Your favourite heroes in real life. _____

Your favourite heroines in real life. _____

Your favourite heroes in fiction. _____

Your favourite heroines in fiction. _____

Your favourite food and drink. _____

Your favourite names. _____

Your pet aversion. _____

What characters in History do you most dislike. _____

What is your present state of mind? _____

For what fault have you most toleration? _____

Your favourite motto. _____

Your chief characteristic. _____

Your favourite qualities in a man. _____

Your favourite qualities in a woman. _____

Your favourite qualities in friends. _____

Your biggest flaw. _____

Your favourite occupation. _____

Your idea of happiness. _____

Your idea of misery. _____

If not yourself, who would you be? _____

Where would you like to live? _____

Your favourite colour and flower. _____

Your favourite prose authors. _____

Your favourite poets. _____

Your favourite heroes in fiction. _____

Your favourite heroines in fiction. _____

Your favourite composers. _____

Your favourite painters. _____

Your favourite heroes in real life. _____

Your favourite heroine in history. _____

Your favourite names. _____

Your pet aversion. _____

What characters in history do you most dislike. _____

The military deed that you admire most. _____

The reform that you appreciate. _____

What gift from nature would you like to have? _____

How would you like to die? _____

What is your present state of mind? _____

For what fault have you most toleration? _____

Your favourite motto. _____

Your chief characteristic. _____

Your favourite qualities in a man. _____

Your favourite qualities in a woman. _____

Your favourite qualities in friends. _____

Your biggest flaw. _____

Your favourite occupation. _____

Your idea of happiness. _____

Your idea of misery. _____

If not yourself, who would you be? _____

Where would you like to live? _____

Your favourite colour and flower. _____

Your favourite prose authors. _____

Your favourite poets. _____

Your favourite heroes in fiction. _____

Your favourite heroines in fiction. _____

Your favourite composers. _____

Your favourite painters. _____

Your favourite heroes in real life. _____

Your favourite heroine in history. _____

Your favourite names. _____

Your pet aversion. _____

What characters in history do you most dislike. _____

The military deed that you admire most. _____

The reform that you appreciate. _____

What gift from nature would you like to have? _____

How would you like to die? _____

What is your present state of mind? _____

For what fault have you most toleration? _____

Your favourite motto. _____

Your favourite virtue. _____

Your favourite qualities in a man. _____

Your favourite qualities in a woman. _____

Your favourite occupation. _____

Your chief characteristic. _____

Your idea of happiness. _____

Your idea of misery. _____

Your favourite colour and flower. _____

If not yourself, who would you be? _____

Where would you like to live? _____

Your favourite prose authors. _____

Your favourite poets. _____

Your favourite painters and composers. _____

Your favourite heroes in real life. _____

Your favourite heroines in real life. _____

Your favourite heroes in fiction. _____

Your favourite heroines in fiction. _____

Your favourite food and drink. _____

Your favourite names. _____

Your pet aversion. _____

What characters in History do you most dislike. _____

What is your present state of mind? _____

For what fault have you most toleration? _____

Your favourite motto. _____

Your favourite virtue. _____

Your favourite qualities in a man. _____

Your favourite qualities in a woman. _____

Your favourite occupation. _____

Your chief characteristic. _____

Your idea of happiness. _____

Your idea of misery. _____

Your favourite colour and flower. _____

If not yourself, who would you be? _____

Where would you like to live? _____

Your favourite prose authors. _____

Your favourite poets. _____

Your favourite painters and composers. _____

Your favourite heroes in real life. _____

Your favourite heroines in real life. _____

Your favourite heroes in fiction. _____

Your favourite heroines in fiction. _____

Your favourite food and drink. _____

Your favourite names. _____

Your pet aversion. _____

What characters in History do you most dislike. _____

What is your present state of mind? _____

For what fault have you most toleration? _____

Your favourite motto. _____

Your chief characteristic. _____

Your favourite qualities in a man. _____

Your favourite qualities in a woman. _____

Your favourite qualities in friends. _____

Your biggest flaw. _____

Your favourite occupation. _____

Your idea of happiness. _____

Your idea of misery. _____

If not yourself, who would you be? _____

Where would you like to live? _____

Your favourite colour and flower. _____

Your favourite prose authors. _____

Your favourite poets. _____

Your favourite heroes in fiction. _____

Your favourite heroines in fiction. _____

Your favourite composers. _____

Your favourite painters. _____

Your favourite heroes in real life. _____

Your favourite heroine in history. _____

Your favourite names. _____

Your pet aversion. _____

What characters in history do you most dislike. _____

The military deed that you admire most. _____

The reform that you appreciate. _____

What gift from nature would you like to have? _____

How would you like to die? _____

What is your present state of mind? _____

For what fault have you most toleration? _____

Your favourite motto. _____

Your chief characteristic. _____

Your favourite qualities in a man. _____

Your favourite qualities in a woman. _____

Your favourite qualities in friends. _____

Your biggest flaw. _____

Your favourite occupation. _____

Your idea of happiness. _____

Your idea of misery. _____

If not yourself, who would you be? _____

Where would you like to live? _____

Your favourite colour and flower. _____

Your favourite prose authors. _____

Your favourite poets. _____

Your favourite heroes in fiction. _____

Your favourite heroines in fiction. _____

Your favourite composers. _____

Your favourite painters. _____

Your favourite heroes in real life. _____

Your favourite heroine in history. _____

Your favourite names. _____

Your pet aversion. _____

What characters in history do you most dislike. _____

The military deed that you admire most. _____

The reform that you appreciate. _____

What gift from nature would you like to have? _____

How would you like to die? _____

What is your present state of mind? _____

For what fault have you most toleration? _____

Your favourite motto. _____

Your favourite virtue. _____

Your favourite qualities in a man. _____

Your favourite qualities in a woman. _____

Your favourite occupation. _____

Your chief characteristic. _____

Your idea of happiness. _____

Your idea of misery. _____

Your favourite colour and flower. _____

If not yourself, who would you be? _____

Where would you like to live? _____

Your favourite prose authors. _____

Your favourite poets. _____

Your favourite painters and composers. _____

Your favourite heroes in real life. _____

Your favourite heroines in real life. _____

Your favourite heroes in fiction. _____

Your favourite heroines in fiction. _____

Your favourite food and drink. _____

Your favourite names. _____

Your pet aversion. _____

What characters in History do you most dislike. _____

What is your present state of mind? _____

For what fault have you most toleration? _____

Your favourite motto. _____

Your favourite virtue. _____

Your favourite qualities in a man. _____

Your favourite qualities in a woman. _____

Your favourite occupation. _____

Your chief characteristic. _____

Your idea of happiness. _____

Your idea of misery. _____

Your favourite colour and flower. _____

If not yourself, who would you be? _____

Where would you like to live? _____

Your favourite prose authors. _____

Your favourite poets. _____

Your favourite painters and composers. _____

Your favourite heroes in real life. _____

Your favourite heroines in real life. _____

Your favourite heroes in fiction. _____

Your favourite heroines in fiction. _____

Your favourite food and drink. _____

Your favourite names. _____

Your pet aversion. _____

What characters in History do you most dislike. _____

What is your present state of mind? _____

For what fault have you most toleration? _____

Your favourite motto. _____

Your chief characteristic. _____

Your favourite qualities in a man. _____

Your favourite qualities in a woman. _____

Your favourite qualities in friends. _____

Your biggest flaw. _____

Your favourite occupation. _____

Your idea of happiness. _____

Your idea of misery. _____

If not yourself, who would you be? _____

Where would you like to live? _____

Your favourite colour and flower. _____

Your favourite prose authors. _____

Your favourite poets. _____

Your favourite heroes in fiction. _____

Your favourite heroines in fiction. _____

Your favourite composers. _____

Your favourite painters. _____

Your favourite heroes in real life. _____

Your favourite heroine in history. _____

Your favourite names. _____

Your pet aversion. _____

What characters in history do you most dislike. _____

The military deed that you admire most. _____

The reform that you appreciate. _____

What gift from nature would you like to have? _____

How would you like to die? _____

What is your present state of mind? _____

For what fault have you most toleration? _____

Your favourite motto. _____

Your chief characteristic. _____

Your favourite qualities in a man. _____

Your favourite qualities in a woman. _____

Your favourite qualities in friends. _____

Your biggest flaw. _____

Your favourite occupation. _____

Your idea of happiness. _____

Your idea of misery. _____

If not yourself, who would you be? _____

Where would you like to live? _____

Your favourite colour and flower. _____

Your favourite prose authors. _____

Your favourite poets. _____

Your favourite heroes in fiction. _____

Your favourite heroines in fiction. _____

Your favourite composers. _____

Your favourite painters. _____

Your favourite heroes in real life. _____

Your favourite heroine in history. _____

Your favourite names. _____

Your pet aversion. _____

What characters in history do you most dislike. _____

The military deed that you admire most. _____

The reform that you appreciate. _____

What gift from nature would you like to have? _____

How would you like to die? _____

What is your present state of mind? _____

For what fault have you most toleration? _____

Your favourite motto. _____

Your favourite virtue. _____

Your favourite qualities in a man. _____

Your favourite qualities in a woman. _____

Your favourite occupation. _____

Your chief characteristic. _____

Your idea of happiness. _____

Your idea of misery. _____

Your favourite colour and flower. _____

If not yourself, who would you be? _____

Where would you like to live? _____

Your favourite prose authors. _____

Your favourite poets. _____

Your favourite painters and composers. _____

Your favourite heroes in real life. _____

Your favourite heroines in real life. _____

Your favourite heroes in fiction. _____

Your favourite heroines in fiction. _____

Your favourite food and drink. _____

Your favourite names. _____

Your pet aversion. _____

What characters in History do you most dislike. _____

What is your present state of mind? _____

For what fault have you most toleration? _____

Your favourite motto. _____

Your favourite virtue. _____

Your favourite qualities in a man. _____

Your favourite qualities in a woman. _____

Your favourite occupation. _____

Your chief characteristic. _____

Your idea of happiness. _____

Your idea of misery. _____

Your favourite colour and flower. _____

If not yourself, who would you be? _____

Where would you like to live? _____

Your favourite prose authors. _____

Your favourite poets. _____

Your favourite painters and composers. _____

Your favourite heroes in real life. _____

Your favourite heroines in real life. _____

Your favourite heroes in fiction. _____

Your favourite heroines in fiction. _____

Your favourite food and drink. _____

Your favourite names. _____

Your pet aversion. _____

What characters in History do you most dislike. _____

What is your present state of mind? _____

For what fault have you most toleration? _____

Your favourite motto. _____

Your chief characteristic. _____

Your favourite qualities in a man. _____

Your favourite qualities in a woman. _____

Your favourite qualities in friends. _____

Your biggest flaw. _____

Your favourite occupation. _____

Your idea of happiness. _____

Your idea of misery. _____

If not yourself, who would you be? _____

Where would you like to live? _____

Your favourite colour and flower. _____

Your favourite prose authors. _____

Your favourite poets. _____

Your favourite heroes in fiction. _____

Your favourite heroines in fiction. _____

Your favourite composers. _____

Your favourite painters. _____

Your favourite heroes in real life. _____

Your favourite heroine in history. _____

Your favourite names. _____

Your pet aversion. _____

What characters in history do you most dislike. _____

The military deed that you admire most. _____

The reform that you appreciate. _____

What gift from nature would you like to have? _____

How would you like to die? _____

What is your present state of mind? _____

For what fault have you most toleration? _____

Your favourite motto. _____

83

Your chief characteristic. _____

Your favourite qualities in a man. _____

Your favourite qualities in a woman. _____

Your favourite qualities in friends. _____

Your biggest flaw. _____

Your favourite occupation. _____

Your idea of happiness. _____

Your idea of misery. _____

If not yourself, who would you be? _____

Where would you like to live? _____

Your favourite colour and flower. _____

Your favourite prose authors. _____

Your favourite poets. _____

Your favourite heroes in fiction. _____

Your favourite heroines in fiction. _____

Your favourite composers. _____

Your favourite painters. _____

Your favourite heroes in real life. _____

Your favourite heroine in history. _____

Your favourite names. _____

Your pet aversion. _____

What characters in history do you most dislike. _____

The military deed that you admire most. _____

The reform that you appreciate. _____

What gift from nature would you like to have? _____

How would you like to die? _____

What is your present state of mind? _____

For what fault have you most toleration? _____

Your favourite motto. _____

Your favourite virtue. ———————————————————————————

Your favourite qualities in a man. ——————————————————

Your favourite qualities in a woman. —————————————————

Your favourite occupation. ———————————————————————

Your chief characteristic. ————————————————————————

Your idea of happiness. ——————————————————————————

Your idea of misery. ————————————————————————————

Your favourite colour and flower. —————————————————————

If not yourself, who would you be? ————————————————————

Where would you like to live? ————————————————————————

Your favourite prose authors. ————————————————————————

Your favourite poets. ————————————————————————————

Your favourite painters and composers. ————————————————————

Your favourite heroes in real life. ————————————————————————

Your favourite heroines in real life. ———————————————————————

Your favourite heroes in fiction. ————————————————————————

Your favourite heroines in fiction. ———————————————————————

Your favourite food and drink. ————————————————————————

Your favourite names. ————————————————————————————

Your pet aversion. ——————————————————————————————

What characters in History do you most dislike. ————————————————

What is your present state of mind? ————————————————————

For what fault have you most toleration? ————————————————————

Your favourite motto. ————————————————————————————

Your favourite virtue. _____

Your favourite qualities in a man. _____

Your favourite qualities in a woman. _____

Your favourite occupation. _____

Your chief characteristic. _____

Your idea of happiness. _____

Your idea of misery. _____

Your favourite colour and flower. _____

If not yourself, who would you be? _____

Where would you like to live? _____

Your favourite prose authors. _____

Your favourite poets. _____

Your favourite painters and composers. _____

Your favourite heroes in real life. _____

Your favourite heroines in real life. _____

Your favourite heroes in fiction. _____

Your favourite heroines in fiction. _____

Your favourite food and drink. _____

Your favourite names. _____

Your pet aversion. _____

What characters in History do you most dislike. _____

What is your present state of mind? _____

For what fault have you most toleration? _____

Your favourite motto. _____

Your chief characteristic. _____

Your favourite qualities in a man. _____

Your favourite qualities in a woman. _____

Your favourite qualities in friends. _____

Your biggest flaw. _____

Your favourite occupation. _____

Your idea of happiness. _____

Your idea of misery. _____

If not yourself, who would you be? _____

Where would you like to live? _____

Your favourite colour and flower. _____

Your favourite prose authors. _____

Your favourite poets. _____

Your favourite heroes in fiction. _____

Your favourite heroines in fiction. _____

Your favourite composers. _____

Your favourite painters. _____

Your favourite heroes in real life. _____

Your favourite heroine in history. _____

Your favourite names. _____

Your pet aversion. _____

What characters in history do you most dislike. _____

The military deed that you admire most. _____

The reform that you appreciate. _____

What gift from nature would you like to have? _____

How would you like to die? _____

What is your present state of mind? _____

For what fault have you most toleration? _____

Your favourite motto. _____

Your chief characteristic. _____

Your favourite qualities in a man. _____

Your favourite qualities in a woman. _____

Your favourite qualities in friends. _____

Your biggest flaw. _____

Your favourite occupation. _____

Your idea of happiness. _____

Your idea of misery. _____

If not yourself, who would you be? _____

Where would you like to live? _____

Your favourite colour and flower. _____

Your favourite prose authors. _____

Your favourite poets. _____

Your favourite heroes in fiction. _____

Your favourite heroines in fiction. _____

Your favourite composers. _____

Your favourite painters. _____

Your favourite heroes in real life. _____

Your favourite heroine in history. _____

Your favourite names. _____

Your pet aversion. _____

What characters in history do you most dislike. _____

The military deed that you admire most. _____

The reform that you appreciate. _____

What gift from nature would you like to have? _____

How would you like to die? _____

What is your present state of mind? _____

For what fault have you most toleration? _____

Your favourite motto. _____

Your favourite virtue. _____

Your favourite qualities in a man. _____

Your favourite qualities in a woman. _____

Your favourite occupation. _____

Your chief characteristic. _____

Your idea of happiness. _____

Your idea of misery. _____

Your favourite colour and flower. _____

If not yourself, who would you be? _____

Where would you like to live? _____

Your favourite prose authors. _____

Your favourite poets. _____

Your favourite painters and composers. _____

Your favourite heroes in real life. _____

Your favourite heroines in real life. _____

Your favourite heroes in fiction. _____

Your favourite heroines in fiction. _____

Your favourite food and drink. _____

Your favourite names. _____

Your pet aversion. _____

What characters in History do you most dislike. _____

What is your present state of mind? _____

For what fault have you most toleration? _____

Your favourite motto. _____

Your favourite virtue. _____

Your favourite qualities in a man. _____

Your favourite qualities in a woman. _____

Your favourite occupation. _____

Your chief characteristic. _____

Your idea of happiness. _____

Your idea of misery. _____

Your favourite colour and flower. _____

If not yourself, who would you be? _____

Where would you like to live? _____

Your favourite prose authors. _____

Your favourite poets. _____

Your favourite painters and composers. _____

Your favourite heroes in real life. _____

Your favourite heroines in real life. _____

Your favourite heroes in fiction. _____

Your favourite heroines in fiction. _____

Your favourite food and drink. _____

Your favourite names. _____

Your pet aversion. _____

What characters in History do you most dislike. _____

What is your present state of mind? _____

For what fault have you most toleration? _____

Your favourite motto. _____

Your chief characteristic. _____

Your favourite qualities in a man. _____

Your favourite qualities in a woman. _____

Your favourite qualities in friends. _____

Your biggest flaw. _____

Your favourite occupation. _____

Your idea of happiness. _____

Your idea of misery. _____

If not yourself, who would you be? _____

Where would you like to live? _____

Your favourite colour and flower. _____

Your favourite prose authors. _____

Your favourite poets. _____

Your favourite heroes in fiction. _____

Your favourite heroines in fiction. _____

Your favourite composers. _____

Your favourite painters. _____

Your favourite heroes in real life. _____

Your favourite heroine in history. _____

Your favourite names. _____

Your pet aversion. _____

What characters in history do you most dislike. _____

The military deed that you admire most. _____

The reform that you appreciate. _____

What gift from nature would you like to have? _____

How would you like to die? _____

What is your present state of mind? _____

For what fault have you most toleration? _____

Your favourite motto. _____

Your chief characteristic. _____

Your favourite qualities in a man. _____

Your favourite qualities in a woman. _____

Your favourite qualities in friends. _____

Your biggest flaw. _____

Your favourite occupation. _____

Your idea of happiness. _____

Your idea of misery. _____

If not yourself, who would you be? _____

Where would you like to live? _____

Your favourite colour and flower. _____

Your favourite prose authors. _____

Your favourite poets. _____

Your favourite heroes in fiction. _____

Your favourite heroines in fiction. _____

Your favourite composers. _____

Your favourite painters. _____

Your favourite heroes in real life. _____

Your favourite heroine in history. _____

Your favourite names. _____

Your pet aversion. _____

What characters in history do you most dislike. _____

The military deed that you admire most. _____

The reform that you appreciate. _____

What gift from nature would you like to have? _____

How would you like to die? _____

What is your present state of mind? _____

For what fault have you most toleration? _____

Your favourite motto. _____

Your favourite virtue. _____

Your favourite qualities in a man. _____

Your favourite qualities in a woman. _____

Your favourite occupation. _____

Your chief characteristic. _____

Your idea of happiness. _____

Your idea of misery. _____

Your favourite colour and flower. _____

If not yourself, who would you be? _____

Where would you like to live? _____

Your favourite prose authors. _____

Your favourite poets. _____

Your favourite painters and composers. _____

Your favourite heroes in real life. _____

Your favourite heroines in real life. _____

Your favourite heroes in fiction. _____

Your favourite heroines in fiction. _____

Your favourite food and drink. _____

Your favourite names. _____

Your pet aversion. _____

What characters in History do you most dislike. _____

What is your present state of mind? _____

For what fault have you most toleration? _____

Your favourite motto. _____

Your favourite virtue. _____

Your favourite qualities in a man. _____

Your favourite qualities in a woman. _____

Your favourite occupation. _____

Your chief characteristic. _____

Your idea of happiness. _____

Your idea of misery. _____

Your favourite colour and flower. _____

If not yourself, who would you be? _____

Where would you like to live? _____

Your favourite prose authors. _____

Your favourite poets. _____

Your favourite painters and composers. _____

Your favourite heroes in real life. _____

Your favourite heroines in real life. _____

Your favourite heroes in fiction. _____

Your favourite heroines in fiction. _____

Your favourite food and drink. _____

Your favourite names. _____

Your pet aversion. _____

What characters in History do you most dislike. _____

What is your present state of mind? _____

For what fault have you most toleration? _____

Your favourite motto. _____

Acknowledgements

The publisher wishes to thank the House of Gérard Darel for the loan of the original copy of *Confessions. An Album to Record Thoughts, Feelings...*, which enabled them to make this book.

The publisher also wishes to thank all the celebrities who kindly answered the Proust Questionnaire: Isabelle Adjani, Rosanna Arquette, Brigitte Bardot, Marisa Berenson, Alain de Botton, Daniel Boulud, Anh Duong, Diane von Furstenberg, Serge Lutens, Richard Meier, Tony Parker, Andrée Putman, Lee Radziwill, Nadine de Rothschild, Luc Sante and Bernar Venet.

Thanks are also due to Jean-Pierre Gillard of the Société des Amis de Marcel Proust et des Amis de Combray, to the illustrator Stéphane Heuet and his publisher, Delcourt, for authorizing the reproduction of a drawing published in the graphic novel *À la Recherche du Temps Perdu*, and to Frankie Rosenblum and assistant Julia Klouse-Farjas of the House of Gérard Darel, and finally, to Philippe Sébirot.

Copyrights

© 2005 Assouline Publishing
601 West 26th Street, 18th floor
New York, NY 10001, USA
Tel.: 212 989-6810   Fax: 212 647-0005
www.assouline.com

Translated introduction from the French by Anne Rubin.

Color separation: Gravor (Switzerland)
Printed in Canada

ISBN: 2 84323 671 1
10 9 8 7 6 5 4 3